The Band

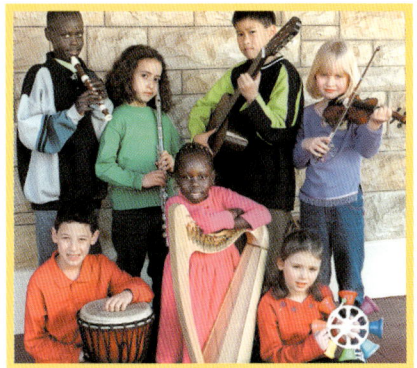

words by Nigel Croser
photographs by Russell Millard

I play the drums.

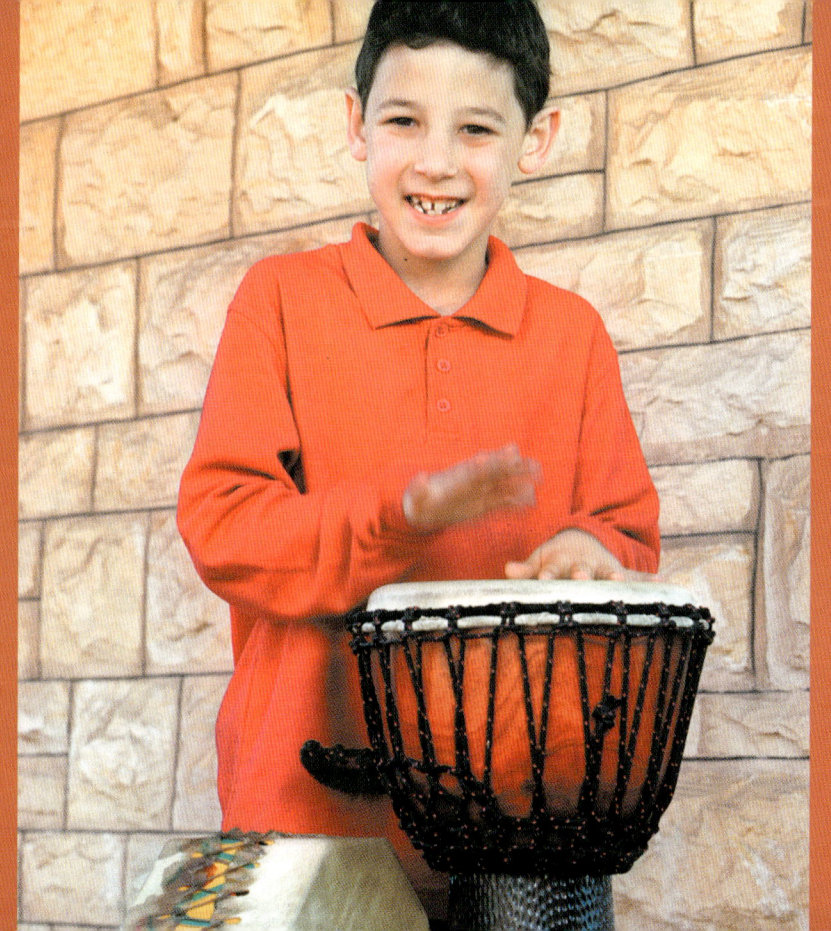

I play the recorder.

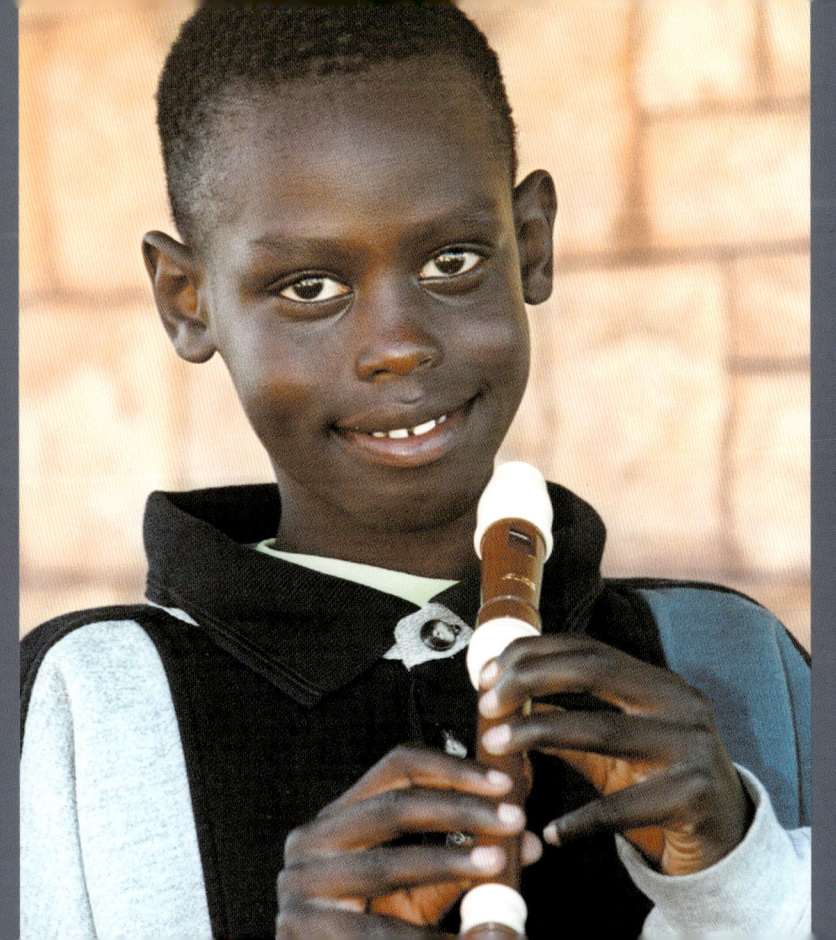

I play the violin.

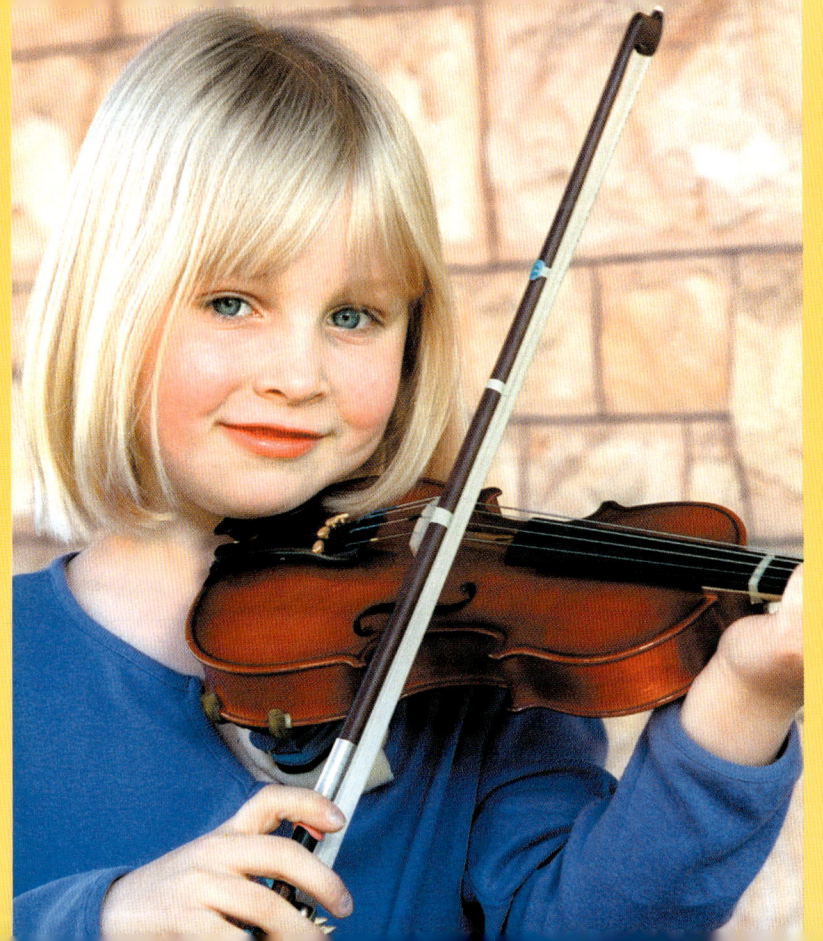

7

I play the bells.

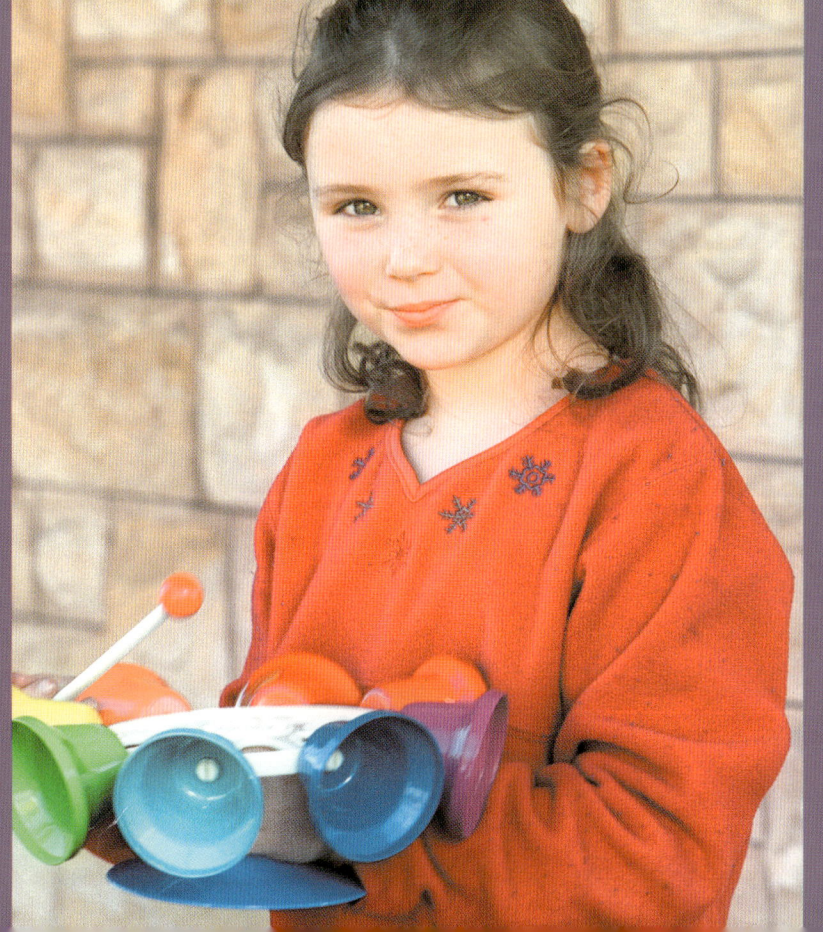

I play the guitar.

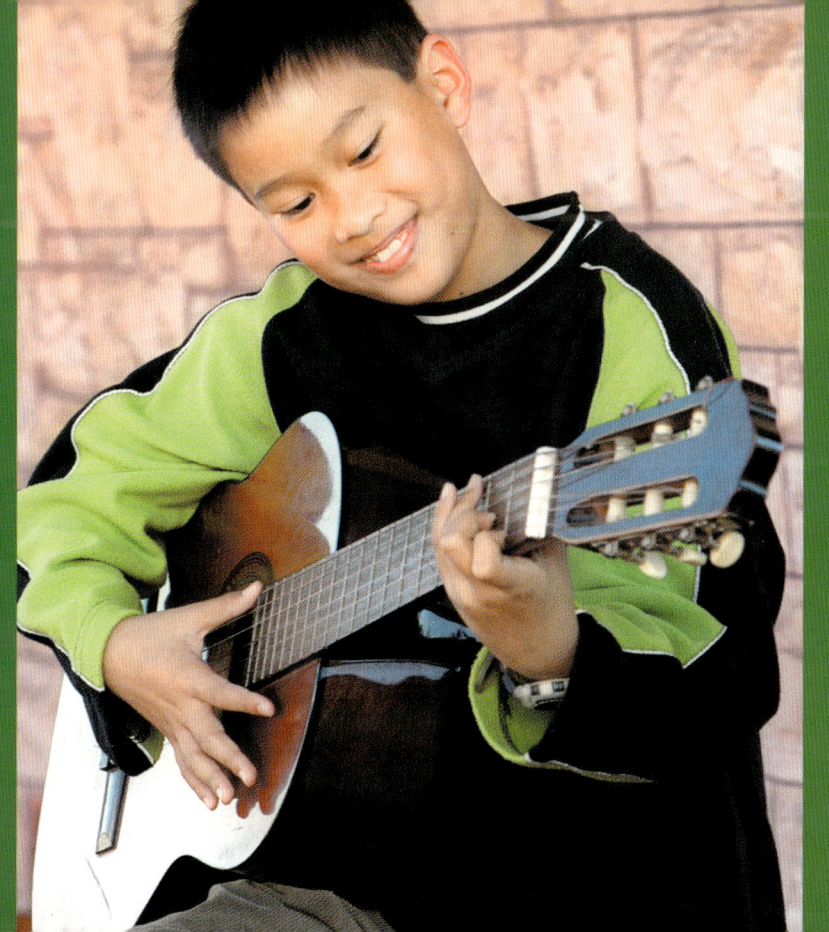

I play the flute.

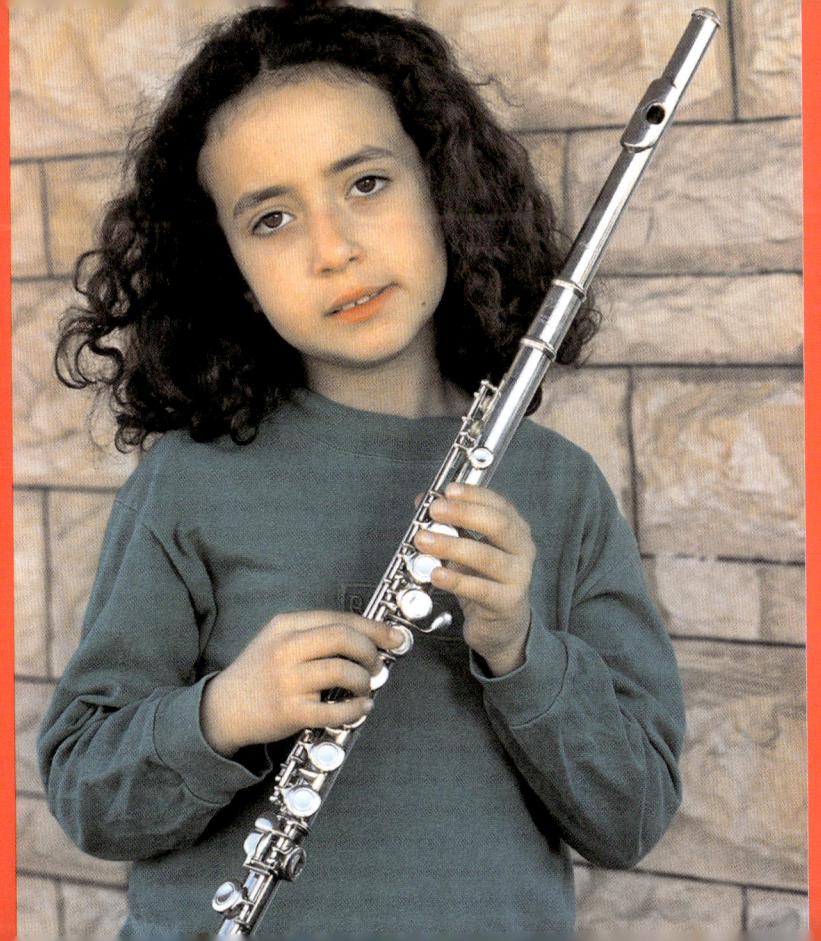

I play the harp.

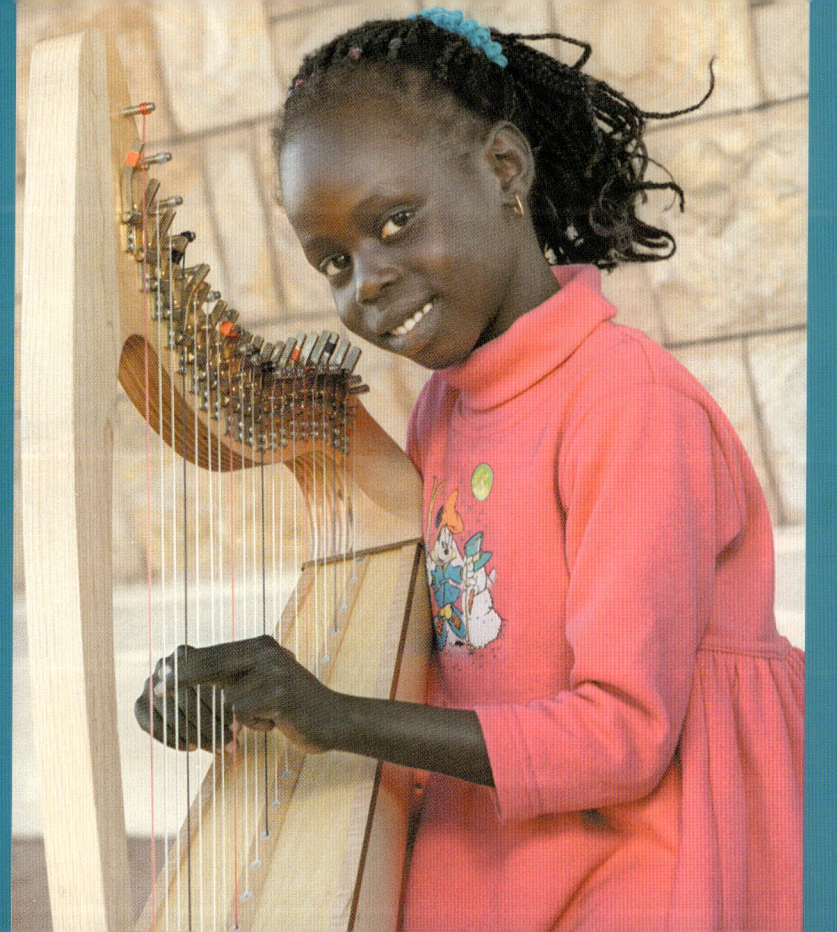

We play together.

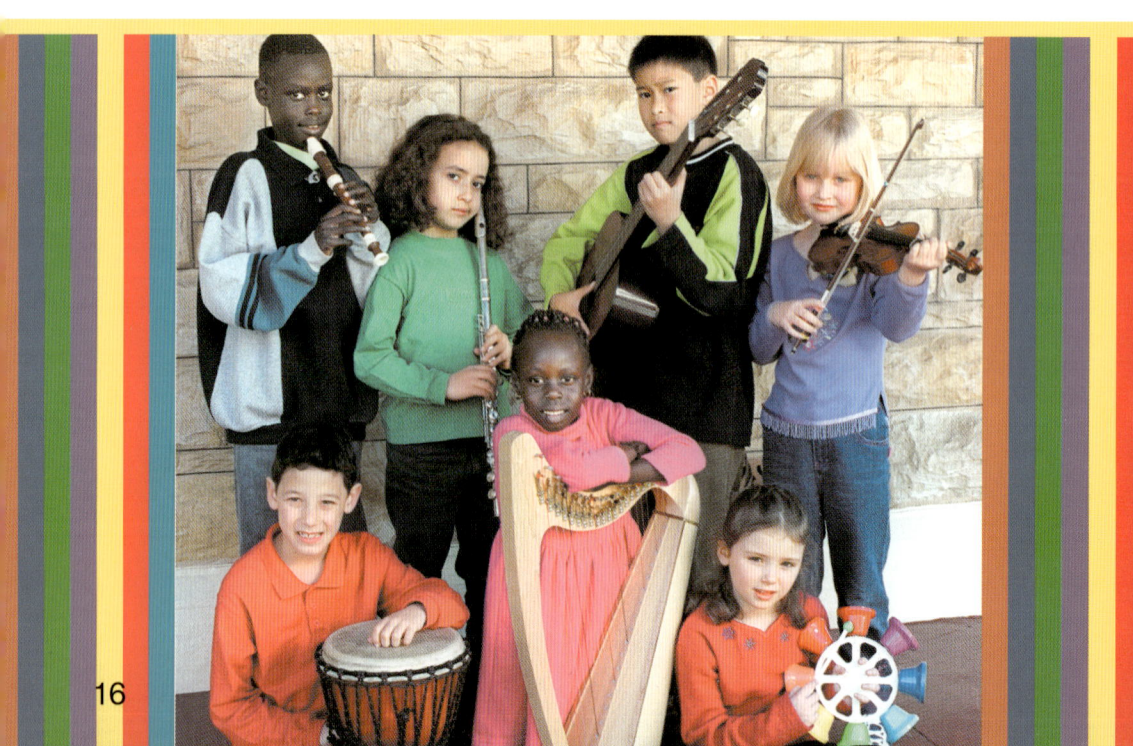